Mark Baxter is a lifelong musician and composer with a passionate love of lang
music to degree level and is a multi-instrumentalist, specialising in piano and guita
performer in both classical and rock music genres. However, his principal musical interest has always
composing, and producing the music and lyrics to songs.

Mark is currently a KS2 primary school teacher, having taught for 20 years in all year groups from ages 6 to 11. Before training as a professional school teacher, he spent eight years as a self-employed piano and music teacher, teaching all ages, and a freelance musician. He has written and produced many projects for his school (Hook-with-Warsash CE Controlled Primary School). Typically, his musicals and musical plays are staged in local professional locations, such as Ferneham Hall in Fareham. Over the years, compositions performed by his choir have featured on local TV and radio; the choir has sung in *Joseph*, featuring Philip Schofield, at the Mayflower Theatre, Southampton; he has sold in excess of 2000 CDs to raise money for Christian Aid and has even made a CD with an ex-manager of Southampton Football Club.

Mark's music has been heard and enjoyed by many pupils and parents and the overwhelming response has been genuinely emotional: it has been often said that the music has a depth and candour that other 'children's' music can lack. Perhaps the appeal is also due to the juxtaposition of musical contrasts. His music has also been highlighted as a major contributor to the moral and spiritual well-being of the pupils in the school in which he teaches (Section 48 inspection May 2007). Mark passionately believes that music can inspire and foster understanding and questioning about the things that really matter to us as humans—the 'big questions' that face all of humanity. He has found that if children are presented with music that addresses these big issues in life, they can respond and develop in a most positive way. He has always endeavoured to write music that questions, challenges and inspires but is based on firmly grounded moral principles.

For further information about Mark's work, visit www.markbaxter.co.uk.

Text copyright © Mark Baxter 2010
The author asserts the moral right
to be identified as the author of this work

Published by
The Bible Reading Fellowship
15 The Chambers, Vineyard
Abingdon OX14 3FE
United Kingdom
Tel: +44 (0)1865 319700
Email: enquiries@brf.org.uk
Website: www.brf.org.uk
BRF is a registered charity

ISBN 978 1 84101 624 5

First published 2010
10 9 8 7 6 5 4 3 2 1 0
All scripture quotations are taken from the Contemporary English Version of
the Bible published by HarperCollins Publishers, copyright © 1991, 1992, 1995
American Bible Society.

A catalogue record for this book is available from the British Library

Printed in Singapore by Craft Print International Ltd

Emmanuel

... assemblies for Christmas

Mark Baxter

A musical and dramatic retelling of the Christmas story

This book is dedicated to my mum and dad, Eileen and Derrick, who inspired me to write music in the first place; and to my wife Heidi and daughter Eloise, who continue that inspiration.

Acknowledgments

With thanks to Chris Hines, friend and head teacher of Hook-with-Warsash CE Controlled Primary School, for his support over the years with this and other musical projects. Thanks, too, to Trevor Reader and his late wife, Lesley. Thanks to the parents, staff and pupils of Hook-with-Warsash for their continued support, and especially the group of Year 6 pupils who sang for the audio recordings. Finally, thanks go to the many people who made this book possible, and especially to Heidi Baxter for her infinite patience and encouragement.

Important information

Photocopy permission

The Copyright Licensing Agency (CLA)

Contents

Foreword

I first met Mark 20 years ago, when he was appointed as a class teacher at Hook-with-Warsash Primary School. His quality as a committed and dedicated teacher quickly became apparent, as did his musical ability.

Over the years, Mark has continued to use his musical talent to give the children at this school some marvellous experiences. They have had the opportunity to perform in the London production of *Joseph and the Amazing Technicolor Dreamcoat* and annually perform a musical written by Mark for three nights in a professional theatre. Shows have included *Scrooge*, *Cinderella*, *White Feather* and *The Snow Queen*. Local schools, being aware of Mark's talent, have often taken the opportunity to perform songs and musicals penned by him.

Mark's music has frequently been used as a fundraising tool for local, national and international charities—for example, performances in local shopping centres and at charity fund-raising events. Without question, the highlights over the years in this area have been the production of CDs sold to raise money for charity. A charity CD in 2004 raised in excess of £2000 for the Tsunami appeal. At the time of writing, a CD has been produced by the school with Mark's music being sung by the staff and children to raise money for Save the Children, for those who have been badly affected by the earthquake in Haiti. The CD has regularly been played on local radio and we hope to raise large sums of money.

As well as secular music, Mark has made major contributions to religious music. He has written musical productions for major Christian festivals, which, again, have been performed in local schools and churches and schools across the country.

All of the above will demonstrate to you the respect and admiration shown to Mark from staff, parents, pupils and all those associated with the school. I am delighted that his talents will now be available to a wider audience through this publication. I feel sure that your children will gain much from performing and singing this work. It will add much to your Christmas celebrations at school and could well become a highlight for schools for many years to come.

Chris Hines
Head Teacher
Hook-with-Warsash CE Controlled Primary School

Introduction

Emmanuel… assemblies for Christmas is a musical and dramatic interpretation of the Christmas story intended for use at Key Stage 2. The material comprises:

- Six ready-to-use assembly outlines
- Follow-up suggestions/reflections for the classroom
- Nativity presentation scripts
- Easy-to-play music scores for all the songs
- Songs and backing tracks available to purchase and download from the website: www.barnabasinschools.org.uk/emmanuel6245.

The material has been developed and performed at Hook-with-Warsash CE Controlled Primary School over a number of years. The resource and the accompanying audio material are designed for use in the following distinctive ways.

- There is a series of five assembly outlines, designed for use in the busy lead-up to Christmas, starting in the first week of Advent. An optional sixth assembly outline is provided to cover Epiphany.
- There is also an alternative, shorter series of presentation readings which can be used in separate assemblies or as a stand-alone act of worship. The latter could comprise an end-of-term presentation in school or service in the local church.

The five scenes of the Christmas narrative form the basis for the five assembly outlines as follows.

Assembly One: God's chosen king

This assembly sets the scene and explains the background to the expectation that God would send his chosen Messiah to rescue the Jewish nation. It takes a brief look at the prophets from Isaiah to John and examines the preparation for Jesus' birth, life, ministry, death and resurrection.

- Bible link: 2 Kings 25:1–12; Isaiah 40:3–5; Isaiah 9:6–7; Luke 1:5–25
- Dramatic presentation: An angel tells about the birth of John the Baptist
- Characters: Jewish people and Babylonians
- Optional introductory song: We are here to sing to you
- Song 1: Take my hand

Assembly Two: The annunciation

This assembly introduces the characters of Mary and Joseph; it briefly explains their relationship to each other, and Jesus' family tree. It then tells the story of the annunciation and Mary's subsequent visit to Elizabeth.

- Bible link: Matthew 1:1–17; Luke 1:26–38; Matthew 1:18–24
- Dramatic presentation: The annunciation and Mary's visit to Elizabeth
- Characters: Angel and Mary
- Song 2: Mary's song

Assembly Three: The journey to Bethlehem

This assembly explains the background to the Roman occupation of Judea, the census decreed by Emperor Augustus and the government of the day. It then goes on to describe Mary and Joseph's journey from Nazareth to Bethlehem and Jesus' birth.

- Bible link: Luke 2:1–7
- Dramatic presentation: Mary and Joseph prepare for their journey. When they arrive, they find no room at the inn and have to make do with a stable for the night.
- Characters: Mary, Joseph, Emperor Augustus, Roman soldiers and innkeepers
- Song 3: Keep on ridin'

Assembly Four: The heavenly host

This assembly sets the background to the shepherds, watching over their flocks in the fields in the hills above the little town of Bethlehem.

- Bible link: Luke 2:8–20
- Dramatic presentation: The angels visit the shepherds, and the shepherds hurry to Bethlehem to find the baby.
- Characters: Angels, shepherds and sheep
- Song 4: Warm winds blowing

Assembly Five: Travellers from afar

This assembly explains what is known about the wise men and their journey to Bethlehem to find the newborn king. The story tells of the gifts the wise men bring and explains the symbolic significance of each gift. It concludes by showing how the ancient prophecy that God's chosen king will be born in Bethlehem is fulfilled.

- Bible link: Matthew 2:1–11; Micah 5:2–5a
- Dramatic presentation: The wise men travel from the east, first to Jerusalem and then to Bethlehem. They bring gifts of gold, frankincense and myrrh to Jesus.
- Characters: Wise men and Herod
- Song 5: Our Lord Emmanuel

Assembly Six (optional): Escape to Egypt

This optional assembly explains the background to Mary and Joseph's escape into Egypt. It tells the story of how the wise men were warned in a dream not to return to King Herod, and shows how Joseph was also warned by an angel of the danger facing his family. The story concludes with the escape into Egypt.

- Bible link: Matthew 2:12–15; Matthew 2:16
- Dramatic presentation: The wise men go home without returning to Herod. Herod orders the killing of baby boys in Bethlehem, and Jesus' family escapes to Egypt.
- Characters: Angel, wise men and Herod
- Song 6: Trust me

Final reflection

At the end of each assembly, there is an opportunity for a time of quiet to think about some of the broader contemporary issues raised. Each reflection is accompanied by a suggestion for an image that could be displayed or projected. Images can be easily sourced on the Internet.

Cue cards

To help the performers, it is suggested that pupils volunteering to play characters in the storyline are given cue cards showing their lines. It is important to choose competent readers, who can be selected either before or during the assembly. The wording for the cue cards can be found on pages 42–43 and can be prepared beforehand by photocopying the words on to paper or card. In some cases, pupils will be required simply to mime as the narrator directs. All volunteers will need to be encouraged to act in character throughout.

Key Bible links

Bible passages are given in full with each assembly outline to show how the story fits with the biblical text. The original Bible texts could be used as part of the assembly or for further study in the classroom.

Taking it further

'Did you know?' facts and ideas for further thought have been included to add interest and promote further investigation. These can be used during the assembly as small cameos presented by pupils, if preparation time allows.

MP3 downloads

The songs and their backing tracks are available to purchase and download from the website: www.barnabasinschools.org.uk/emmanuel6245

Ready-to-use assembly outlines

God's chosen king

This assembly sets the scene and explains the background to the Old Testament expectation that God would send his chosen king to rescue his people from the oppression they continually experienced from neighbouring nations. It takes a brief look at the prophets from Isaiah to John the Baptist and examines the preparation for Jesus' birth, life and ministry, as well as his death and resurrection.

You will need

- To learn the optional introductory song 'We are here to sing to you'.
- To learn the song 'Take my hand'. The harmony part will need to be learnt thoroughly and independently before the parts are put together. (Consider this a golden rule for all the songs with harmony parts.)
- Several pupils to mime as the people of Israel and two pupils to mime as Babylonians.
- For the final reflection, a photograph of a modern contemporary war situation involving an 'occupied' territory—for example, showing an occupying soldier or tank with local children.
- Cue cards for Assembly One, photocopied from page 42.

Key Bible links

In Zedekiah's ninth year as king, on the tenth day of the tenth month, King Nebuchadnezzar of Babylonia led his entire army to attack Jerusalem. The troops set up camp outside the city and built ramps up to the city walls.

After a year and a half, all the food in Jerusalem was gone. Then on the ninth day of the fourth month, the Babylonian troops broke through the city wall. That same night, Zedekiah and his soldiers tried to escape through the gate near the royal garden, even though they knew the enemy had the city surrounded. They headed toward the desert, but the Babylonian troops caught up with them near Jericho. They arrested Zedekiah, but his soldiers scattered in every direction. Zedekiah was taken to Riblah, where Nebuchadnezzar put him on trial and found him guilty…

About a month later, in Nebuchadnezzar's nineteenth year as king, Nebuzaradan, who was his official in charge of the guards, arrived in Jerusalem. Nebuzaradan burned down the Lord's temple, the king's palace, and every important building in the city, as well as all the houses. Then he ordered the Babylonian soldiers to break down the walls around Jerusalem. He led away as prisoners the people left in the city, including those who had become loyal to Nebuchadnezzar. Only some of the poorest people were left behind to work the vineyards and the fields.
2 KINGS 25:1–12

Someone is shouting: 'Clear a path in the desert! Make a straight road for the Lord our God. Fill in the valleys; flatten every hill and mountain. Level the rough and rugged ground. Then the glory of the Lord will appear for all to see. The Lord has promised this!'
ISAIAH 40:3–5

A child has been born for us. We have been given a son who will be our ruler. His names will be Wonderful Adviser and Mighty God, Eternal Father and Prince of Peace. His power will never end; peace will last for ever. He will rule David's kingdom and make it grow strong. He will always rule with honesty and justice. The Lord All-Powerful will make certain that all of this is done.
ISAIAH 9:6–7

When Herod was king of Judea, there was a priest called Zechariah from the priestly group of Abijah. His wife Elizabeth was from the family of Aaron. Both of them were good people and pleased the Lord God by obeying all that he had commanded. But they did not have children. Elizabeth could not have any, and both Zechariah and Elizabeth were already old.

One day Zechariah's group of priests were on duty, and he was serving God as a priest. According to the custom of the priests, he had been chosen to go into the Lord's temple that day and to burn incense, while the people stood outside praying.

All at once an angel from the Lord appeared to Zechariah at the right side of the altar. Zechariah was confused and afraid when he saw the angel. But the angel told him: 'Don't be afraid, Zechariah! God has heard your prayers. Your wife Elizabeth will have a son, and you must name him John. His birth will make you very happy, and many people will be glad. Your son will be a great servant of the Lord...'

Zechariah said to the angel, 'How will I know this is going to happen? My wife and I are both very old.' The angel answered, 'I am Gabriel, God's servant, and I was sent to tell you this good news. You have not believed what I have said. So you will not be able to say a thing until all this happens. But everything will take place when it is supposed to.'

The crowd was waiting for Zechariah and kept wondering why he was staying so long in the temple. When he did come out, he could not speak, and they knew he had seen a vision. He motioned to them with his hands, but did not say a thing.

When Zechariah's time of service in the temple was over, he went home. Soon after that, his wife was expecting a baby, and for five months she did not leave the house. She said to herself, 'What the Lord has done for me will keep people from looking down on me.'

LUKE 1:5–15A AND 18–25

Taking it further

Did you know?

- The word 'Emmanuel' means 'God with us'.
- Nebuchadnezzar was king of Babylon at the time of the fall of Jerusalem.
- Isaiah probably lived in Jerusalem in the eighth century BC. He was married with two sons, and his name means 'The Lord saves!'

Ideas for further thought

- Who were the other kings of Israel?
- What was the 'Golden Age'?
- Who built the first great temple in Jerusalem?
- What is a prophet? Is it someone who predicts the future, or something else? Can you name other biblical prophets?

Script: God's chosen king

All children and staff enter to the backing recording of 'Take my hand'.

Narrator: Welcome, everyone, to *Emmanuel!*, an exciting dramatisation of the story of Jesus' birth told in music, readings and mime.

Song: We are here to sing to you (optional)

Narrator: We will start our story some 600 years before the first Christmas—about 2600 years ago. Now, I need some people to take the role of the Jewish people from that time, and two more to be Babylonians.

Narrator chooses three or four volunteers.

Narrator: Once, long, long ago, in a land east of the Mediterranean Sea, the Jewish people were living happily in their own kingdom. For generations they had a good life and were ruled by great kings such as King David and King Solomon. They were prosperous and very contented.

Several children mime the people being happy.

Narrator: People served one God, instead of many as others had done in the past.

The children mime praying in different directions, then all face and pray the same way.

The biggest city in Israel, and the centre of the Jewish religion, was Jerusalem. It was a magnificent city—the people's pride and joy.

Children mime pride—blowing on clenched hands, polishing nails on lapels and so on.

However, this happiness was not to last, because the kingdom of Israel became divided over the centuries. At last, Jerusalem was invaded and the temple destroyed. Terrible hardship and war followed and, in the end, the people found themselves exiled to the north-east—to Babylon.

Babylonians mime using whips to move the Jewish people across the stage area. The people look troubled.

Narrator: The Jewish people had lost everything, and now they were in exile, far from home.

Jewish people: We remember the good old days. If only there was someone from David's line to help us now!

Narrator: Well, a long time passed and the people were eventually allowed to go back home. They rebuilt the city of Jerusalem but they still longed for the days of old when the great kings had ruled. They remembered, through wonderful stories, the golden days long past. They told beautiful tales of King Solomon and of how the young David had slain the giant Goliath. They recalled how David became a fair and just king. They longed for someone who would come to return them to their former happiness.

Jewish people: We remember the good old days. If only there was someone from David's line to help us now!

Narrator: At the same time, the writings of the wisest of men did indeed

 Reproduced with permission from *Emmanuel… assemblies for Christmas* published by BRF 2010 (978 1 84101 624 5) www.barnabasinschools.org.uk

speak of just such a man. A day would come, they wrote, when someone from David's line would come. God would send his chosen person to lead the people to freedom and back to where they belonged.

Jewish people: We remember the good old days. If only there was someone from David's line to help us now!

Narrator: These men who wrote about what would happen in the future were called 'prophets'. (In those days, women and girls were not really allowed to do this sort of thing.) One very famous prophet, called Isaiah, wrote that people should get ready for the coming of God's chosen king. He said they should clear the way for a new king. The people were filled with hope!

More time passed. The centuries rolled by and now the people were living in a divided kingdom under Roman occupation. Once again they were oppressed, this time by the mighty Roman Empire. The words of Isaiah echoed in their minds as, yet again, their expectation grew of being rescued by someone sent by God.

Now at this time there lived an old Jewish priest called Zechariah, and his wife, Elizabeth. They had been good and devout people but they had never been blessed with children. Everyone thought that they were too elderly to have children—but they were wrong! An angel appeared to Zechariah and told him that he would have a son. Elizabeth would become pregnant! This son would be called John and he would prepare the way for the coming of Jesus. He would become known as John the Baptist and, like the prophets of old, he spread the word that people should get ready because God's chosen king was coming. He was coming very soon! Someone was coming at last! John was the one who would indeed prepare the way for Jesus.

Someone was coming to save them! Emmanuel! God with us!

Song: Take my hand

Reflection
A picture of a contemporary war situation is projected or shown.

Narrator: As we approach Christmas, we might reflect on the idea that we sometimes ignore the wisdom of the past and messages from history, particularly times of war. As we are gathered here, there are people whose countries are occupied by foreign forces. We could consider the faith of those who never give up believing that salvation is possible. Just as Zechariah and Elizabeth discovered in our story, there is always hope.

That's the end of our assembly. As you leave, I hope that you can take hope with you from this story. In the words of a famous actor, Christopher Reeve, 'Once you choose hope, anything's possible.'

All staff and pupils leave to a reprise of 'Take my hand'.

The annunciation

The story introduces us to Mary and Joseph. It reminds us of Jesus' family tree and then describes the angel's visit to Mary. After hearing the angel's news, Mary goes to visit her cousin Elizabeth.

You will need

- To learn the song 'Mary's song' (this piece is most effective if a suitable soloist can be used for one of the verses).
- A photograph of a mother and newborn baby for the reflection.
- Cue cards for Assembly Two, photocopied from page 42.

Key Bible links

Jesus Christ came from the family of King David and also from the family of Abraham. And this is a list of his ancestors. From Abraham to King David, his ancestors were: Abraham, Isaac, Jacob, Judah and his brothers (Judah's sons were Perez and Zerah, and their mother was Tamar), Hezron; Ram, Amminadab, Nahshon, Salmon, Boaz (his mother was Rahab), Obed (his mother was Ruth), Jesse, and King David.

From David to the time of the exile in Babylonia, the ancestors of Jesus were: David, Solomon (his mother had been Uriah's wife), Rehoboam, Abijah, Asa, Jehoshaphat, Jehoram; Uzziah, Jotham, Ahaz, Hezekiah, Manasseh, Amon, Josiah, and Jehoiachin and his brothers.

From the exile to the birth of Jesus, his ancestors were: Jehoiachin, Shealtiel, Zerubbabel, Abiud, Eliakim, Azor, Zadok, Achim; Eliud, Eleazar, Matthan, Jacob, and Joseph, the husband of Mary, the mother of Jesus, who is called the Messiah.

There were fourteen generations from Abraham to David. There were also fourteen from David to the exile in Babylonia and fourteen more to the birth of the Messiah.

MATTHEW 1:1–17

One month later God sent the angel Gabriel to the town of Nazareth in Galilee with a message for a virgin named Mary. She was engaged to Joseph from the family of King David. The angel greeted Mary and said, 'You are truly blessed! The Lord is with you.'

Mary was confused by the angel's words and wondered what they meant. Then the angel told Mary, 'Don't be afraid! God is pleased with you, and you will have a son. His name will be Jesus. He will be great and will be called the Son of God Most High. The Lord God will make him king, as his ancestor David was. He will rule the people of Israel for ever, and his kingdom will never end.'

Mary asked the angel, 'How can this happen? I am not married!' The angel answered, 'The Holy Spirit will come down to you, and God's power will come over you. So your child will be called the holy Son of God. Your relative Elizabeth is also going to have a son, even though she is old. No one thought she could ever have a baby, but in three months she will have a son. Nothing is impossible for God!'

Mary said, 'I am the Lord's servant! Let it happen as you have said.' And the angel left her.

LUKE 1:26–38

This is how Jesus Christ was born. A young woman named Mary was engaged to Joseph from King David's family. But before they were married, she learned that she was going to have a baby by God's Holy Spirit. Joseph was a good man and did not want to embarrass Mary in front of everyone. So he decided to call off the wedding quietly.

While Joseph was thinking about this, an angel from the Lord came to him in a dream. The angel said, 'Joseph, the baby that Mary will have is from the Holy Spirit. Go ahead and marry her. Then after her baby is born, name him Jesus, because he will save his people from their sins.' So the Lord's promise came true, just as the prophet had said, 'A virgin will have a baby boy, and he will be called Immanuel', which means 'God is with us'.

After Joseph woke up, he and Mary were soon married, just as the Lord's angel had told him to do.

MATTHEW 1:18–24

Taking it further

Did you know?

- The word *Messiah* comes from the Hebrew language and means 'anointed'. In Greek, the word for 'anointed' is *Christos*, from which we get the word 'Christ'.
- Joseph may have been a carpenter, but there is no direct evidence that this was his profession.
- Mary's real name was Miriam: Mary is the Greek version of the name.

Ideas for further thought

- Why was it so important for Matthew to show us that Jesus was a member of the Jewish faith, descended from King David himself?
- Mary's song of praise is known as the 'Magnificat' because this word means 'glorifies' in Latin. There are some very famous musical versions of the Magnificat. The one written by Bach is one of the best-known.
- John the Baptist was the last person to prophesy about Jesus. He was a wild character who was said to eat grasshoppers and honey.

Script: The annunciation

Narrator: *(Use this narration if the assembly follows on from Assembly One)* Welcome to the second part of the story of Emmanuel. You may remember, last time, hearing about the Jewish people's longing that God would send someone to rescue them from the oppression they experienced from neighbouring countries. The prophet Isaiah said that God would send his chosen person. This person would be someone from King David's family: he would be the rescuer that the people were waiting for.

Narrator: *(Use this narration if this is your first Christmas assembly)* Today's story is about one of the most special moments in anyone's life. I wonder how many of you will have children of your own when you are older? *(Allow time for interaction)*

Narrator: *(Continue from here)* Many people fall in love and decide to live their lives together. Lots of people make the decision to start a family. This is the story of a young girl who lived around 2000 years ago, who was planning to do just that. Her name was Mary and she was engaged to be married to a man called Joseph, but things didn't go quite as she had planned. Joseph was a descendant of one of the great kings of Israel—King David. Mary was at home, probably daydreaming about her forthcoming marriage, when something extraordinary happened.

Now I need two volunteers: one to be Mary and one to be an angel.

Narrator chooses two suitable volunteers and gives them the appropriate cue cards showing the words they need to say.

Narrator: The angel said to Mary,

Angel: *(From cue card)* You are truly blessed! The Lord is with you.

Narrator: Mary was terrified; she didn't know what he meant.

Mary looks terrified.

Angel: *(From cue card)* Don't be afraid! God is pleased with you, and you will have a son. His name will be Jesus. He will be great and will be called the Son of God Most High. The Lord God will make him king, as his ancestor David was. He will rule the people of Israel for ever, and his kingdom will never end.

Narrator: But Mary still did not understand. How could she give birth to a son? She wasn't married yet!

Mary: *(From cue card)* How can this happen? I am not married!

Angel: *(From cue card)* The Holy Spirit will come down to you, and God's power will come over you. So your child will be called the holy Son of God. Your relative Elizabeth is also going to have a son, even though she is old. No one thought she could ever have a baby, but in three months she will have a son. Nothing is impossible for God!

Narrator: Mary at last understood. She fell to her knees and said…

 Reproduced with permission from *Emmanuel… assemblies for Christmas* published by BRF 2010 (978 1 84101 624 5) www.barnabasinschools.org.uk

Mary:	*(From cue card)* I am the Lord's servant! Let it happen as you have said.
Narrator:	And with that, the angel left.
	The two volunteers return to their seats.
Narrator:	Well, how might Mary have felt? What should she do?
	Allow time for children to respond.
Narrator:	A short time later, Mary went to see her cousin, Elizabeth. Elizabeth's husband, Zechariah, had also had a visit from an angel—and Elizabeth was expecting a baby, even though she was quite elderly at the time. Mary and Elizabeth must have been a great support for each other.
	Mary stayed with Elizabeth for the next three months until Elizabeth's son John was born. After this, Mary returned home.
	We'll join Mary in singing 'Mary's song' as she thinks about the life that lies ahead for her and her son.
	Song: Mary's song
	Reflection *A photograph of a mother and baby is projected or displayed.*
Narrator:	As we think about how Mary must have been feeling, let's consider the feelings of parents everywhere, and especially mothers, who so often have a special love for their children.

As a final thought as we part, a wise man once observed that every baby who has ever been born started life knowing absolutely no evil. Even a person who does terrible things when he or she grows up begins life as a pure and innocent baby.

The music for 'Mary's song' is played and the song may be sung again as the children exit.

The journey to Bethlehem

This assembly explains that Mary and Joseph's country, Judea, was occupied by soldiers who were part of the vast Roman Empire. The Jewish people were therefore subject to Roman rule. It tells how the Emperor Augustus ordered that there should be a census, which required every citizen to return to the town or city of their birth. This meant that Mary and Joseph had to journey from Nazareth to Bethlehem. The assembly finishes with the story of Jesus' birth.

You will need

- To learn the song 'Keep on ridin''. (If you include the harmony bridge sections, follow the golden rule and learn the parts separately. Put them together only when they are known thoroughly.)
- Volunteers to play the parts of Mary, Joseph, Emperor Augustus and three or four innkeepers.
- A cardboard laurel crown for Augustus.
- A map showing the extent of the Roman Empire at the time (to be projected or displayed if you wish).
- For the reflection, a photograph of refugees today, travelling with all their belongings.
- Cue cards for Assembly Three, photocopied from page 42.

Key Bible link

About that time Emperor Augustus gave orders for the names of all the people to be listed in record books. These first records were made when Quirinius was governor of Syria.

Everyone had to go to their own home town to be listed. So Joseph had to leave Nazareth in Galilee and go to Bethlehem in Judea. Long ago Bethlehem had been King David's home town, and Joseph went there because he was from David's family.

Mary was engaged to Joseph and travelled with him to Bethlehem. She was soon going to have a baby, and while they were there, she gave birth to her firstborn son. She dressed him in baby clothes and laid him on a bed of hay, because there was no room for them in the inn.

LUKE 2:1–7

Taking it further

Did you know?

- The month of July was named after Julius Caesar, and August was named after Augustus.
- There is actually no inn mentioned in the Bible. The word *kataluma* is the word used, which would usually be translated as 'guest room'.
- There is no mention of a stable, either. In those days, a feeding trough (manger) could well have been in the main downstairs living-room of a simple dwelling.

Ideas for further thought

- Had the Roman Empire not been run in such an organised and efficient way, Jesus would not have been born in Bethlehem. So the authoritarian Roman Empire affected Jesus' life even before his birth (his birthplace was chosen by Roman order), and was later instrumental in his untimely and brutal death.
- The word often translated as 'inn' in Luke 2:7 (*kataluma*) is the same word that is used for the room in which the last supper was held (Luke 22:12). So much of our understanding depends on translation! Do you know in which language the Gospel of Luke was written?

Script: The journey to Bethlehem

Narrator: Welcome to the story of Mary and Joseph's journey to Bethlehem. We find Mary and Joseph both shocked but thrilled and excited at the prospect of becoming new parents. Imagine how they felt! The angel's visits had prepared them in some ways, though we must remember that things were very different in those days. Mary and Joseph did not have the same freedom that we perhaps take for granted. In what way might they not have been free?

The narrator deals with responses and steers the discussion towards the Roman occupation of the Mediterranean countries.

Narrator: That's right, at this time the Roman Empire stretched from north Africa in the south, west to Portugal, east to Jerusalem and, by the end of the first century, north into Britain.

If possible, display or project a large map to show the extent of the Roman Empire and the location of Nazareth and Bethlehem.

Narrator: Mary and Joseph's country was occupied, which meant that there were Roman soldiers making sure that people kept the Roman law. Now, I'll need some soldiers…

The narrator chooses a small number of volunteers.

Narrator: *(To the volunteers, in a 'sergeant major' voice)* Eyes front! Shoulders back! There was no slouching in the Roman army! Now, you 'orrible lot! Who's your boss? Who gives the orders?

The volunteers probably will not know.

Narrator: *(Addressing the whole assembly)* Right, the rest of you… Who was in charge of these 'ere Romans?

The narrator steers responses towards 'the Emperor' or 'Caesar'.

Narrator: Yes! And don't you forget it. The Emperor—you may know him. Full name: Gaius Julius Caesar Augustus. He took over Rome soon after his great-uncle died. You've definitely heard of him—great-uncle Julius Caesar.

The narrator selects a pupil who can read well and with confidence, and invites him or her to put on the laurel crown.

Narrator: Hail, Caesar Augustus!

All: *(Saluting Roman-style with raised hand)* Hail, Caesar Augustus!

Augustus: *(From cue card)* I decree that there shall be a census! Every adult shall return to the town of their birth to be counted. All shall obey! By decree of the mighty Augustus!

All: Hail, Caesar!

The narrator thanks and dismisses the child playing the part of Augustus.

Narrator: And so everyone had to return to their town of birth to be registered in the Roman census. Mary and Joseph had to set off on the journey from the town of Nazareth in Galilee, all the way to the town of Bethlehem in Judea, even though Mary was ready to have her baby.

The narrator chooses volunteers to play Mary, Joseph and three or four innkeepers.

Narrator: Mary and Joseph set off on the long journey, probably carrying a few belongings and some food and water. Perhaps they had a donkey, but the Bible doesn't say that they did.

Let's sing our song, 'Keep on ridin'', in a Country and Western style, and imagine we are trying to keep our spirits up on a long journey.

Mary and Joseph mime going on their journey while the song is being sung.

Song: Keep on ridin'

Narrator: At last the weary couple reached the town of Bethlehem. They began to knock on doors to find a room to stay in, because they were both exhausted and the time for Mary to have her baby was getting nearer and nearer.

Joseph: *(From cue card)* Do you have anywhere for us to stay? We have travelled a long way and the time for Mary's baby to be born is getting close.

Innkeeper: *(From cue card)* Sorry, no room here…

Joseph's question may be repeated two or three times, with the same response from three or four different innkeepers.

Narrator: Well, you can imagine how Mary and Joseph felt! They were exhausted, hungry, thirsty and tired. Nearly at their wits' end, they came to a small and humble-looking dwelling. They were so desperate, they knocked and waited—and at last the door opened.

Joseph: *(From cue card, addressing narrator)* Do you have anywhere for us to stay? We have travelled a long way and the time for Mary's baby to be born is getting close.

Narrator: *(Speaking as an innkeeper)* Why, no rooms as such, no! The whole town is full, you see, because of the census. But you look desperate! I'll tell you what—if you don't mind the animals, you can stay down here with them. It's a bit cramped and smelly, but you look as if you need to rest.

The narrator guides Mary and Joseph to sit down.

Narrator: And so Mary and Joseph found room at last—in a humble stable in Bethlehem among the animals. There was no cradle in such a place, but Mary laid baby Jesus in a manger. And that was how the Son of God was born—in the lowest of lowly surroundings with no fuss or ceremony. He lay peacefully sleeping in an animals' feeding trough, with his loving mother and proud father looking on. The breathing and snuffling of the animals in the stable carried on in the background, the creatures unaware that they were the sole witnesses of the birth of the Son of God.

Reflection

A picture of refugees on a journey with their belongings should be displayed or projected.

Narrator: We might think about all those who have to make difficult journeys in life, or those who find the journey of life difficult at times. As we think about Jesus being born in a stable among the animals, we might reflect on the difference between the circumstances of Jesus' birth and our own celebrity culture. The person who had most influence on the history of the world came into that world in the most humble and lowly circumstances imaginable.

Finally, as a parting thought about individual freedom, it has been said that 'for every person who lives without freedom, the rest of us must face the guilt'.

The music to 'Keep on ridin'' is played as the children exit.

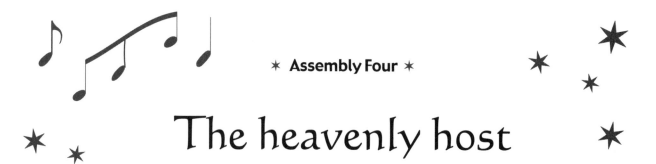

★ Assembly Four ★

The heavenly host

This assembly tells the story of the shepherds who were watching their flocks in the fields in the hills above Bethlehem, of the angels who appeared to them and of the shepherds' rush to see the newborn baby.

You will need:

- To learn the song 'Warm winds blowing'. (The harmony is very easy to learn if you follow the golden rule of learning the parts separately and thoroughly before putting them together.)
- A candle and matches or lighter.
- Simple dressing-up clothes (optional). For example, four teatowel-style headdresses, four sheets with head holes, possibly a set of sheep masks, some tinsel and white sheet angel costumes.
- Volunteers to be shepherds and angels. (The narrator needs to choose and prepare the angels before the assembly so that they can be ready dressed in whatever 'angelic' costume is available.)
- Musical chimes (optional).
- Cue cards for Assembly Four, photocopied from page 42.

Key Bible link

That night in the fields near Bethlehem some shepherds were guarding their sheep. All at once an angel came down to them from the Lord, and the brightness of the Lord's glory flashed around them. The shepherds were frightened. But the angel said, 'Don't be afraid! I have good news for you, which will make everyone happy. This very day in King David's home town a Saviour was born for you. He is Christ the Lord. You will know who he is, because you will find him dressed in baby clothes and lying on a bed of hay.'

Suddenly many other angels came down from heaven and joined in praising God. They said: 'Praise God in heaven! Peace on earth to everyone who pleases God.'

After the angels had left and gone back to heaven, the shepherds said to each other, 'Let's go to Bethlehem and see what the Lord has told us about.' They hurried off and found Mary and Joseph, and they saw the baby lying on a bed of hay.

When the shepherds saw Jesus, they told his parents what the angel had said about him. Everyone listened and was surprised. But Mary kept thinking about all this and wondering what it meant.

As the shepherds returned to their sheep, they were praising God and saying wonderful things about him. Everything they had seen and heard was just as the angel had said.

LUKE 2:8–20

Taking it further

Did you know?

- Some experts say that it is possible to graze sheep on the hills around Bethlehem only from March to November. This doesn't mean that the Christmas story isn't true—just that the actual timing of Jesus' birth would probably have been between those months.
- The story of the shepherds is in Luke's Gospel.

Ideas for further thought

- Some historians believe that Jesus may have been born in any year between 6BC and AD4, which is the year when Herod died.

Script: The heavenly host

Pupils and staff enter to the recorded version of 'Warm winds blowing' without vocals.

Narrator: Our build-up to Christmas continues!

The narrator may question children about their preparations for Christmas.

Narrator: We are all busy getting ready for Christmas, what with buying presents and making sure we don't miss anybody out, getting the shopping done—and all that food! There's a turkey to buy, Christmas pudding to make, and all our usual work to fit in as well. It really is difficult!

The jobs that people did when Jesus was born were often quite different from the jobs most people do today. Some people were shepherds…

The narrator chooses four pupils to be shepherds and gives each one a headdress and other dressing-up items.

Narrator: And I think we need some sheep!

The narrator chooses volunteers and gives each one a sheep mask.

Narrator: So here are our shepherds and their grazing sheep…

The narrator encourages the shepherds and sheep to mime the story.

Narrator: Night is falling and the shepherds decide to make camp on a hillside for the night. The hillside is on some high ground next to the small village of Bethlehem.

The narrator sits the shepherds and sheep down quietly and calmly. If possible, the lights can be dimmed.

Narrator: This night is one of those lovely calm and beautiful nights that you sometimes get in warm countries. In those days, there was no noise from cars or aeroplanes—no engines or motors of any sort. And there was also no light pollution—no orange glow of street lights glaring across the sky, and no headlights. The brightest thing you would see would probably be the campfire. Surely the shepherds must have wondered at the beautiful stars hanging in the heavens. Everything was calm.

A candle is lit and placed where it can be clearly seen.

Narrator: Let's look at our candle and pretend we are on the hillside near Bethlehem that night, as if we were looking into the flames of the campfire and thinking.

As we do so, let us sing our shepherds' song, 'Warm winds blowing', and think about the shepherds just doing their ordinary day-in, day-out job. Imagine how peaceful it must have been for them that night.

Song: Warm winds blowing

After the song, the lights are put on full again and the narrator directs the first angel to face the shepherds.

Narrator:	Suddenly there is a dazzling light. The shepherds are afraid—they can hear music. The sheep are very frightened, too!

A musical effect, such as chimes, could be used here.

Angel:	(*From cue card*) Don't be afraid! I have good news for you, which will make everyone happy! This very day in King David's home town a Saviour was born for you. He is Christ the Lord! You will know who he is, because you will find him dressed in baby clothes and lying on a bed of hay.

The other angels join the first angel.

Angels:	(*From cue card*) Praise God in heaven! Peace on earth to everyone who pleases God.

The angels exit.

Narrator:	The shepherds hurried to find Mary and Joseph and saw the baby lying on a bed of hay. They knelt down in wonder. They told Mary and Joseph what the angels had said. Mary must have found it amazing to hear their news. She kept thinking about what it all might mean. Then the shepherds returned to their sheep in a state of great happiness. They praised God and said wonderful things about him. They must have wondered why God had chosen them to be the first to see baby Jesus. Everything had happened exactly as the angel had described.

Reflection

An image of a contemporary Palestinian shepherd may be displayed or projected.

Narrator:	As we sit here now, there are shepherds tending their sheep as in the old days. We might consider them poor by our materialistic standards. Something to think about is that, whatever jobs we might do, like the shepherds, none of us knows the true significance of our lives.

Let's thank our actors and give them a big round of applause. As we go out, perhaps we could think about the angel's news about the baby who was to change the history of the world— and that the very first people to visit him were ordinary people, just like us.

The candle is extinguished and pupils exit to the music of 'Warm winds blowing'.

 Reproduced with permission from *Emmanuel… assemblies for Christmas* published by BRF 2010 (978 1 84101 624 5) www.barnabasinschools.org.uk

Travellers from afar

This assembly introduces the wise men and tells the story of their journey to Bethlehem to see the newborn king. It briefly mentions their encounter with Herod and explains the symbolic significance of each of the gifts they gave to Jesus. Finally, it shows how the ancient prophecy that God's chosen king would be born in Bethlehem is fulfilled.

You will need

- To learn the song 'Our Lord Emmanuel'. (The two parts of the song are very easy to learn: just follow the golden rule of learning the parts separately and thoroughly before putting them together.)
- Three volunteers to act as the wise men and one to be Herod. (Herod needs to be someone who doesn't mind playing the part of the villain.)
- For the reflection, either a photograph of a melting glacier or iceberg (representing global warming), a photograph of a nuclear explosion or a picture of Albert Einstein.
- Cue cards for Assembly Five, photocopied from page 43.

Key Bible links

When Jesus was born in the village of Bethlehem in Judea, Herod was king. During this time some wise men from the east came to Jerusalem and said, 'Where is the child born to be king of the Jews? We saw his star in the east and have come to worship him.'

When King Herod heard about this, he was worried, and so was everyone else in Jerusalem. Herod brought together the chief priests and the teachers of the Law of Moses and asked them, 'Where will the Messiah be born?'

They told him, 'He will be born in Bethlehem, just as the prophet wrote, "Bethlehem in the land of Judea, you are very important among the towns of Judea. From your town will come a leader, who will be like a shepherd for my people Israel."'

Herod secretly called in the wise men and asked them when they had first seen the star. He told them, 'Go to Bethlehem and search carefully for the child. As soon as you find him, let me know. I want to go and worship him too.'

The wise men listened to what the king said and then left. And the star they had seen in the east went on ahead of them until it stopped over the place where the child was. They were thrilled and excited to see the star.

When the men went into the house and saw the child with Mary, his mother, they knelt down and worshipped him. They took out their gifts of gold, frankincense, and myrrh and gave them to him.

MATTHEW 2:1–11

Bethlehem Ephrath, you are one of the smallest towns in the nation of Judah. But the Lord will choose one of your people to rule the nation—someone whose family goes back to ancient times. The Lord will abandon Israel only until this ruler is born, and the rest of his family returns to Israel. Like a shepherd taking care of his sheep, this ruler will lead and care for his people by the power and glorious name of the Lord his God. His people will live securely, and the whole earth will know his true greatness, because he will bring peace.

MICAH 5:2–5A

Taking it further

Did you know?

- In the Bible, it doesn't specify how many wise men there were. The traditional number of three is based on the fact that there were three gifts.
- The wise men were actually astrologers.
- There is no mention of camels in the Bible. The camels are probably a Christmas card invention, based on the fact that this is a common mode of transport in the Near East.

Ideas for further thought

- In reality, the journey of the wise men probably took weeks, months or even years. In the Bible, Jesus is described as a child, not a baby, when they eventually arrive in Bethlehem. Also, Mary and Joseph are living in a house by this time.
- The names Caspar, Melchior and Balthazar come from legend built up around the story of the wise men.

Script: Travellers from afar

Narrator: As Christmas gets closer and we near the end of our Christmas story, let's start our assembly today by singing the song, 'Our Lord Emmanuel'.

Song: Our Lord Emmanuel

Narrator: In our last assembly, we heard the story of how angels appeared to shepherds on a hillside near Bethlehem. We saw how the shepherds, who were just ordinary folk, were the first people to visit the newborn baby. Today, we see how the three wise men fit into the story.

To help with the story, I need three wise men and I need someone to play King Herod.

The narrator chooses three volunteers to play the three wise men, and someone to play Herod—possibly a teacher.

Narrator: *(To the wise men)* Now, listen carefully and remember that you are wise men. So try to look wise! Jesus was born in the small town of Bethlehem in Judea, where Herod was king. Some time after Jesus' birth, wise men from the east arrived at King Herod's palace in Jerusalem and asked…

The narrator directs the three wise men to process across the stage and read from their cue cards.

Wise men: *(From cue card)* Where is the child born to be king of the Jews? We saw his star in the east and have come to worship him.

Narrator: When King Herod heard about this, he was worried, and so was everyone else in Jerusalem. Herod brought together the chief priests and the teachers of the Law of Moses and asked them:

Herod: *(From cue card)* Where will the Messiah be born?

Narrator: He was told, 'He will be born in Bethlehem, just as the prophet wrote, "Bethlehem in the land of Judea, you are very important among the towns of Judea. From your town will come a leader, who will be like a shepherd for my people Israel."'

Herod secretly called the wise men to him and asked them when they had first seen the star. He said…

Herod: *(From cue card)* Go to Bethlehem and search carefully for the child. As soon as you find him, let me know. I want to go and worship him too.

Narrator: So the wise men set off, still following the star, which appeared to move ahead of them. They followed it until it came to rest over the place where Jesus was.

The narrator motions to the wise men to process and kneel before an imaginary Jesus.

 Reproduced with permission from *Emmanuel… assemblies for Christmas* published by BRF 2010 (978 1 84101 624 5) www.barnabasinschools.org.uk

Narrator:	Here they gave him their gifts of gold, frankincense and myrrh.

The three wise men read out the symbolic significance of their gifts.

Wise man 1:	*(From cue card)* Gold—the most precious and noble metal. It doesn't rust or tarnish and stays always bright, the true gift for a king.
Wise man 2:	*(From cue card)* Frankincense— burnt to release its scented smoke. A symbol of life and rejuvenation.
Wise man 3:	*(From cue card)* Myrrh—used in the embalming process, to prepare the body after death. A symbol of Jesus' own death, even at his birth!
Narrator:	Thus, the ancient prophecy that God's chosen king would be born in Bethlehem was fulfilled. And there we leave the story of the wise men. They had delivered their gifts and recognised Jesus' kingship. He had now been acknowledged not just by the simple shepherds but by the wisest of the wise.

Reflection
Display or project either a photograph of a melting glacier or iceberg (representing global warming), a photograph of a nuclear explosion or a picture of Albert Einstein.

Narrator:	We might pause to consider the wise people of our time—the scientists and politicians who make decisions that affect us all. We could think about the enormous responsibility they have to use their power and knowledge in the right ways, particularly at this time when the biggest threat to humankind is people themselves.

Song: Our Lord Emmanuel (optional reprise)

Reproduced with permission from *Emmanuel… assemblies for Christmas* published by BRF 2010 (978 1 84101 624 5) www.barnabasinschools.org.uk

Assembly Six (optional)

Escape to Egypt

This optional assembly is about King Herod's threat to Mary, Joseph and Jesus, and how they had to escape the danger posed by him. It tells how the wise men were warned in a dream not to return to Herod, and also how Joseph was warned by an angel of the danger facing the family. It ends with the story of Joseph's escape to Egypt with Mary and Jesus.

You will need

- To learn the song 'Trust me'. (Also prepare 'Take my hand' if desired for the end.)
- A volunteer to play King Herod (the person chosen for Assembly Five would be ideal).
- A volunteer to play an angel (one speaking line) and three wise men (mime only).
- For the reflection, a photograph of Hitler addressing the crowds at a Nuremberg Rally, if possible juxtaposed with an image of Gandhi.
- Cue cards for Assembly Six, photocopied from page 43.

Key Bible links

Later they were warned in a dream not to return to Herod, and they went back home by another road.

After the wise men had gone, an angel from the Lord appeared to Joseph in a dream and said, 'Get up! Hurry and take the child and his mother to Egypt! Stay there until I tell you to return, because Herod is looking for the child and wants to kill him.'

That night, Joseph got up and took his wife and the child to Egypt, where they stayed until Herod died. So the Lord's promise came true, just as the prophet had said, 'I called my son out of Egypt.'

When Herod found out that the wise men from the east had tricked him, he was very angry. He gave orders for his men to kill all the boys who lived in or near Bethlehem and were two years old and younger. This was based on what he had learnt from the wise men.

MATTHEW 2:12–16

Taking it further

Did you know?

- Herod was a weak and dangerous king, who ruthlessly murdered anyone who he thought was a threat to his position.
- There were many kings called 'Herod' at the time. After his arrest, Jesus was brought to stand trial before another King Herod—Herod Antipas, the son of Herod the Great (Luke 23:6–12).

Ideas for further thought

- Herod's instruction to kill all the baby boys under the age of two may mean that it could have taken the wise men up to two years to reach their destination.

Script: Escape to Egypt

Narrator: The Bible tells us that in the days of King Herod, Jesus was born in the small town of Bethlehem in Judea. We have heard the stories of the shepherds and the wise men, and learnt about the gifts that the wise men brought Jesus. The Christmas story ends, though, not with the visit of the wise men, but with an escape under cover of darkness from the ruthless plans of King Herod.

King Herod was known as 'Herod the Great'. He carried out impressive building programmes, including the rebuilding of the temple in Jerusalem. But he was a highly unpopular ruler, mainly because he would stop at nothing to make safe his position as king. It was not a good idea to upset King Herod if you wanted to stay alive—something we need to bear in mind as we learn about this last part of the Christmas story.

The narrator introduces the volunteer who will play the part of King Herod.

Herod: *(Reading angrily from the cue card)* I've heard about a new king being born somewhere in Bethlehem—and I don't like it! I will *not* have a threat to my royal throne! This new king is in deep trouble! Even if I have to kill all the baby boys in the area, there shall be no king but me!

Narrator: Can anyone remember what Herod did in the last assembly?

Narrator allows time for response.

Narrator: That's right! He sent the wise men off to find the newborn king and ordered them to let him know where the baby was, so that he too could worship him. Let's have some wise men…

The narrator chooses the wise men and instructs them to process across the front of the hall.

Herod: *(From cue card)* Go to Bethlehem and search carefully for the child. As soon as you find him, let me know. I want to go and worship him too.

Narrator: But the wise men were worried— they did not really trust King Herod. As they journeyed on to see Jesus, their concern grew and at night they had nightmares about what Herod would do. Our song today tells the story of what the wise men dreamt about.

Song: Trust me

The narrator sets the wise men up as if they are to return to King Herod across the available space.

Narrator: Now we know that King Herod was prepared to let nothing stand in the way of his position as king, even to the point of getting rid of a young child who he saw as a threat. He must have been desperate to hear news from the wise men and he waited impatiently for them to return— but they did not come back to the palace. Their dreams had rightly made them suspicious of King Herod. They knew that he would think nothing of killing the baby… and perhaps them too! So they went home by a different road.

The narrator directs the wise men to act with much head-shaking and frowning, changing their minds and going back to their seats.

Narrator: I wonder how Herod reacted to being let down by the wise men. Yes, he was angry! He was furious! But an angel was on hand to make sure that Jesus was kept safe.

The narrator chooses a volunteer to play the angel.

Narrator: After the visit by the wise men, Mary and Joseph probably had no idea that they were in danger. But, as they slept, an angel appeared to Joseph in a dream and said...

Angel: *(From cue card)* Get up! Hurry and take the child and his mother to Egypt! Stay there until I tell you to return, because Herod is looking for the child and wants to kill him.

Narrator: When Herod found out that the wise men from the east had tricked him, he was very angry. He gave orders for his men to kill all the boys who lived in or near Bethlehem and were two years old and younger. This was based on what he had learnt from the wise men. But, that night, under cover of darkness, Joseph had taken Mary and Jesus and quietly left Bethlehem. The little family journeyed to Egypt, where they stayed until Herod died.

Reflection
Display or project a photograph of Hitler addressing the crowds at a Nuremberg Rally, if possible juxtaposed with an image of Gandhi.

Narrator: Power can change people. King Herod became obsessed with his own power, which led to his terrible actions. History is littered with examples of people whose lust for power has brought misery and death to millions of others. But some people use the power they have for the good of everyone.

Our journey is over and our Christmas story told. It's the story of Emmanuel, 'God with us'. Whatever our beliefs, the story encourages us to bring a little light into the world, and love and peace to those around us.

Song: Take my hand (optional repeat on dismissal)

 Reproduced with permission from *Emmanuel... assemblies for Christmas* published by BRF 2010 (978 1 84101 624 5) www.barnabasinschools.org.uk

Follow-up suggestions and reflections for the classroom

Assembly One: God's chosen king

Year 3

- Design an invitation, asking all your friends and family to a party for a very special visitor.
- Draw a simple timeline going back to the time of Isaiah's prophecy, through to Jesus' birth and up to today. Find out the relative times between those important dates.

Year 4

- Pretend to be Zechariah. What thoughts would you put down on paper?
- Think about what it would be like if you could not speak. How would you act out the news that Zechariah received in the temple.

Year 5

- Discuss Zechariah's jobs at the temple. What jobs have to be done in a modern-day church (cleaning brasses, gardening and so on)? Write out a job description for someone to help with jobs in a modern-day church.
- Create a class Advent calendar. Use a whole display board and draw relevant pictures for the 24 windows.

Year 6

- Discuss the dilemma of whether we should always tell the truth. Do we sometimes need to tell lies to protect people?
- Research how Advent is celebrated around the world. Compare and contrast your discoveries with what happens in Britain.

Assembly Two: The annunciation

Year 3

- Hold a discussion about how Mary might have felt before, during and after the visit from the angel. How might her emotions have changed?
- Draw a series of portraits showing the different emotions that Mary may have felt.

Year 4

- Draw Mary's visit to Elizabeth. Write in speech bubbles what they might have said to each other.
- As a class, draw, paint or make a collage of an angel. Then think of words describing the qualities that an angel would need to have. Write ideas on Post-it notes and stick them around the angel.

Year 5

- Write a diary entry about Mary's thoughts and feelings after the angel's visit, having heard the news that she was to be Jesus' mother.
- Discuss how Mary would have felt when she heard Elizabeth's news (disbelief, joy, happiness, worry and so on).

Year 6

- Discuss moments in your life when everything has felt perfect. Write down your personal thoughts and share them if you wish.
- Research paintings of the annunciation. Try to recreate your favourite picture 'live' and take a photo of it. Compare the photo to the original artwork.

Assembly Three: The journey to Bethlehem

Year 3

- Carry out research work on the donkey. Write a report about a donkey.
- In Geography, discuss how you could travel from Nazareth to Bethlehem today. How long would it take? How long would it have taken on a donkey?

Year 4

- Write a list of instructions on how to look after a donkey.
- Carry out research on the weather in Israel in December. Compare your findings to the weather in the UK during the same month.

Year 5

- Find out about Bethlehem and write up a tourist pamphlet for it.
- Find a map of Europe and colour in the extent of the Roman Empire 2000 years ago.

Year 6

- Write a play script showing the conversation that Mary and Joseph might have had as they tried to find a room for the night.
- How long would the journey from Nazareth to Bethlehem have taken by donkey 2000 years ago? How many miles per day can a donkey travel? If you were to travel 80 miles from your school, which towns could you reach? (Use Google Earth.)

Assembly Four: The heavenly host

Year 3

- Discuss how the shepherds' feelings might have changed during the visit of the angels (such as 'calm to excitement' or 'fear to curiosity'). Gather your ideas and create a poem expressing these mixed feelings.
- Present your poems graphically on a computer, perhaps writing a poem within the outline of an angel or decorating it with small angels, Christian symbols and so on.

Year 4

- After discussion, write a report for a newspaper, describing the shepherds' meeting with the angels. Include newspaper conventions such as a headline, 'sensationalist' narrative and first-person eyewitness accounts.
- Dress up some angels and shepherds and 'pose' the scene as if it has been captured by press photographers. Photograph it yourself and include it in a computer presentation of a newspaper story.

Year 5

- Discuss different possible 'points of view' of the same incident, then write two short diary entries about the 'heavenly host' incident. These could show the feelings of a shepherd who is excited, yet trusting, contrasted with one who is overwhelmed and fearful.
- Paint pictures of faces showing the different emotions felt by the shepherds, and perhaps 'dress' them with fabric and beards. The pictures could be used to make a class display.

Year 6

- Discuss how Luke's Gospel includes the birth of Jesus in a lowly stable. Why is this significant? Why were ordinary shepherds from the fields chosen as the first people to visit Jesus?
- Write the story of the shepherds' experiences using descriptive language: try to include what they felt as well as what they heard and saw.
- Discuss contrasts in visual art. Paint a watercolour wash background representing the evening sky in a mixture of colours, and stick on cut-out silhouettes of the shepherds, sheep and hillside in black. Perhaps silver, gold or white angels could be added.

Assembly Five: Travellers from afar

Year 3

- Write a list of words to describe what it might be like to ride a camel. Use a thesaurus to help.
- Paint a picture of the special present you would give to a newborn king. Discuss reasons why you chose that particular gift.

Year 4

- Carry out research on camels and present your findings to the class.
- Research the significance of gold, frankincense and myrrh. Are any of these substances still used today?

Year 5

- Find out about modern-day astrologers. What do they do?
- Look at constellations. Try to make up your own pictures using the stars.

Year 6

- Produce a piece of persuasive writing, encouraging your friend to follow a star and go on a long journey.
- In Maths, make a three-dimensional star (with six pyramid shapes stuck to a cube).

Assembly Six (optional) Escape to Egypt

Year 3

- Find as many words as possible to describe King Herod. Use a thesaurus to help.
- Create pictographs of words that describe King Herod.

Year 4

- Discuss how you would escape from someone who was unkind to you in the playground. How would you handle it? Who would you ask to help you?
- Look at maps to see where Joseph, Mary and Jesus escaped from and where they fled to.

Year 5

- Carry out research about Herod the Great.
- Imagine you are Mary or Joseph and discuss who you would tell if you had to escape in secret. Why would you tell that person? How would you tell them?

Year 6

- Discuss how people have had to escape from their countries and homelands because of other people's evil attitudes or actions (for example, refugees, evacuees, people of a particular faith or race, and so on.)
- Imagine you are an evacuee. Write a diary entry expressing your thoughts and feelings once you have reached your destination.

Presentation scripts

This dramatic presentation is intended to be used either as the basis for five or six shorter, alternative assemblies requiring minimal preparation, or as a stand-alone complete version of the Christmas story, achieved by running the acts into one whole performance. In the latter case, a traditional nativity could be acted out as required, with the spoken lines being performed by actors. This could comprise an end-of-term presentation in school or a service in the local church.

Stage directions have been deliberately omitted as each acting situation and context will be individual. The scripts can be tailored easily to meet individual requirements.

Act One: God's chosen king

Bible link

When Herod was king of Judea, there was a priest called Zechariah from the priestly group of Abijah. His wife Elizabeth was from the family of Aaron. Both of them were good people and pleased the Lord God by obeying all that he had commanded. But they did not have children. Elizabeth could not have any, and both Zechariah and Elizabeth were already old.

One day Zechariah's group of priests were on duty, and he was serving God as a priest. According to the custom of the priests, he had been chosen to go into the Lord's temple that day and to burn incense, while the people stood outside praying.

All at once an angel from the Lord appeared to Zechariah at the right side of the altar. Zechariah was confused and afraid when he saw the angel. But the angel told him: 'Don't be afraid, Zechariah! God has heard your prayers. Your wife Elizabeth will have a son, and you must name him John. His birth will make you very happy, and many people will be glad. Your son will be a great servant of the Lord…'

Zechariah said to the angel, 'How will I know this is going to happen? My wife and I are both very old.' The angel answered, 'I am Gabriel, God's servant, and I was sent to tell you this good news. You have not believed what I have said. So you will not be able to say a thing until all this happens. But everything will take place when it is supposed to.'

The crowd was waiting for Zechariah and kept wondering why he was staying so long in the temple. When he did come out, he could not speak, and they knew he had seen a vision. He motioned to them with his hands, but did not say a thing.

When Zechariah's time of service in the temple was over, he went home. Soon after that, his wife was expecting a baby, and for five months she did not leave the house. She said to herself, 'What the Lord has done for me will keep people from looking down on me.'

LUKE 1:5–15A AND 18–25

Script

Optional song: We are here to sing to you

Reader 1: Welcome to *Emmanuel!*, our dramatic presentation of the Christmas story, which we will tell you using music, drama and readings. It is a story filled with inspiration and hope. We hope you enjoy it.

Reader 2: Our story starts long ago, when Herod was king of Judea. Now the coming of God's chosen king had long since been foretold, and it was written that his birth would take place in Bethlehem. However, the first part of our story is not about the birth of Jesus but the arrival of another baby, who would grow up to be the man who prepared the way for Jesus. This man was called John: he was Jesus' cousin.

Reader 1: At this time, about 2000 years ago, there was a priest called Zechariah who lived with his wife

Elizabeth. Both Zechariah and Elizabeth were quite elderly—probably what we would call late middle-aged. They had devoted their lives to their work and, though they were content in many ways, both were unhappy that God had never blessed their marriage with children. As the years passed, their sadness grew: they would grow old and lonely without the support of any sons or daughters.

Reader 2: This even made them feel angry sometimes. Zechariah would speak in dark tones, saying things like 'Why has God never blessed us with children? Have we not worked hard all our lives in his service?' Even though she too felt the emptiness in her life, Elizabeth would comfort him with words such as 'Ours is not to reason why God has chosen this for us, Zechariah—but there is always hope!'

Reader 1: Now, one day, Zechariah was working in the temple, burning incense while the people outside prayed. This was part of his duty as a priest. Suddenly, he saw an angel! The angel was standing to the right of the altar, in front of his very eyes. Zechariah was confused. Then the angel said…

Reader 2: Don't be afraid, Zechariah! God has heard your prayers. Your wife Elizabeth is going to have a son, and you must name him John. Your son will be a great servant of God and the Holy Spirit will guide him. John will lead many people in Israel to turn back to their God. He will go ahead of the Lord and make people ready. People who now disobey God will begin to worship him properly and John will get people ready for the Lord.

Reader 1: Zechariah was amazed. He didn't believe the angel, and said…

Reader 2: How can this happen? My wife and I are both very old.

Reader 1: The angel replied…

Reader 2: I am the angel Gabriel and I was sent by God to tell you this good news. But I can tell that you have not believed me. As a punishment for your lack of faith, you will not be able to speak until all that I have said will happen has happened.

Reader 1: Zechariah emerged from the temple and stumbled toward the crowds, who could see that he was shocked and in a state of high emotion. But, as the angel had said, he couldn't speak. He made gestures with his hands and eventually managed to make clear what had happened. Zechariah returned home and Elizabeth did indeed become pregnant, despite her age. They were filled with joy and the people they knew were very happy for them. Their prayers had been answered.

Reader 2: And so it was that God sent the angel Gabriel to earth to bring the news of John the Baptist's birth. John was the one who would prepare the way for Jesus.

Song: Take my hand

Act Two: The annunciation

Bible links

One month later God sent the angel Gabriel to the town of Nazareth in Galilee with a message for a virgin named Mary. She was engaged to Joseph from the family of King David. The angel greeted Mary and said, 'You are truly blessed! The Lord is with you.'

Mary was confused by the angel's words and wondered what they meant. Then the angel told Mary, 'Don't be afraid! God is pleased with you, and you will have a son. His name will be Jesus. He will be great and will be called the Son of God Most High. The Lord God will make him king, as his ancestor David was. He will rule the people of Israel for ever, and his kingdom will never end.'

Mary asked the angel, 'How can this happen? I am not married!'

The angel answered, 'The Holy Spirit will come down to you, and God's power will come over you. So your child will be called the holy Son of God. Your relative Elizabeth is also going to have a son, even though she is old. No one thought she could ever have a baby, but in three months she will have a son. Nothing is impossible for God!'

Mary said, 'I am the Lord's servant! Let it happen as you have said.' And the angel left her.

LUKE 1:26–38

This is how Jesus Christ was born. A young woman named Mary was engaged to Joseph from King David's family. But before they were married, she learned that she was going to have a baby by God's Holy Spirit. Joseph was a good man and did not want to embarrass Mary in front of everyone. So he decided to call off the wedding quietly.

While Joseph was thinking about this, an angel from the Lord came to him in a dream. The angel said, 'Joseph, the baby that Mary will have is from the Holy Spirit. Go ahead and marry her. Then after her baby is born, name him Jesus, because he will save his people from their sins.'

So the Lord's promise came true, just as the prophet had said, 'A virgin will have a baby boy, and he will be called Immanuel,' which means 'God is with us.'

After Joseph woke up, he and Mary were soon married, just as the Lord's angel had told him to do.

MATTHEW 1:18–24

* * *

Script

Reader 2: Six months after the angel Gabriel had visited Zechariah to tell him that his wife, though elderly, would have a child who was to prepare the way for Jesus, Mary found that she too was expecting a baby.

Reader 1: A young carpenter called Joseph was engaged to a young girl called Mary. There was nothing exceptional about this couple, even though Joseph was a descendant of King David. Everything seemed to be going to plan: the engagement was announced and Mary and Joseph were looking forward to their wedding day. Then Mary had a visit from the angel Gabriel, and learnt that she had been chosen to be the mother of God's Son: she was going to have a very special baby. The angel greeted Mary and said…

Reader 2: You are truly blessed! The Lord is with you.

Reader 1: Mary was confused by the angel's words and wondered what they meant. Then the angel told Mary…

Reader 2: Don't be afraid! God is pleased with you, and you will have a son. His name will be Jesus. He will be great and will be called the Son of God Most High. The Lord God will make him king, as his ancestor David was. He will rule the people of Israel for ever, and his kingdom will never end.

Reader 1: Mary asked the angel, 'How can this happen? I am not married!' The angel answered…

 Reproduced with permission from *Emmanuel… assemblies for Christmas* published by BRF 2010 (978 1 84101 624 5) www.barnabasinschools.org.uk

Reader 2:	The Holy Spirit will come down to you, and God's power will come over you. So your child will be called the holy Son of God. Your relative Elizabeth is also going to have a son, even though she is old. No one thought she could ever have a baby, but in three months she will have a son. Nothing is impossible for God!
Reader 1:	Mary said, 'I am the Lord's servant! Let it happen as you have said.' And the angel left her.
Reader 2:	When Joseph heard Mary's news, he was deeply troubled. Joseph was a good man and did not want to embarrass Mary in front of everyone, so he decided to call off the wedding quietly. While Joseph was thinking about this, an angel from the Lord came to him in a dream. The angel said…
Reader 1:	Joseph, the baby that Mary will have is from the Holy Spirit. Go ahead and marry her. Do not worry! Then, after her baby is born, name him Jesus.
Reader 2:	The angel continued…
Reader 1:	Mary's baby boy will be called 'Immanuel', which means 'God with us'.
Reader 2:	When Joseph awoke, he understood what the dream had meant and he decided to do what the angel had said. Soon, Joseph and Mary were married.

Song: Mary's song

Act Three: The journey to Bethlehem

Bible link

About that time Emperor Augustus gave orders for the names of all the people to be listed in record books. These first records were made when Quirinius was governor of Syria.

Everyone had to go to their own home town to be listed. So Joseph had to leave Nazareth in Galilee and go to Bethlehem in Judea. Long ago Bethlehem had been King David's home town, and Joseph went there because he was from David's family.

Mary was engaged to Joseph and travelled with him to Bethlehem. She was soon going to have a baby, and while they were there, she gave birth to her firstborn son. She dressed him in baby clothes and laid him on a bed of hay, because there was no room for them in the inn.

LUKE 2:1–7

Script

Reader 1:	Even though Mary was going to have a very special baby, she and Joseph were just an ordinary couple living in a small part of the mighty Roman Empire. Shortly before Mary's baby was due, the Roman Emperor, Caesar Augustus, announced that there was going to be a census of the people and everyone had to return to the town of their birth.
Reader 2:	Everyone had to go to their own home town to be counted. Joseph was a descendant of King David and Bethlehem had been King David's home town, so Joseph had to leave Nazareth in Galilee and go to Bethlehem in Judea. It was a journey of some 80 miles.
Reader 1:	Joseph and Mary set off with the few things they needed for the journey. Mary would probably have ridden on a donkey, with Joseph leading the way to Bethlehem. The journey would

be long and dangerous, but the Roman law had to be obeyed.

Song: Keep on ridin'

Reader 1:   At last they arrived in Bethlehem, tired and anxious to find somewhere to stay before Mary's baby arrived. But the town was packed! Everyone had arrived for the census. Time and again they were turned away. 'No room here!' would be the all-too-familiar cry. At last, when they had nearly given up hope, Joseph knocked on one more door and asked for a room. The owner replied, 'Well, not a room as such, but if you don't mind the animals, you can share their stall.'

Reader 2:   And so Mary and Joseph settled down among the animals. At least it was warm and dry. That night, Jesus was born. He lay peacefully sleeping in a bed of hay, with his loving mother looking on. The animals' breath was warm and calm: they were unaware that they were the sole witnesses of Jesus' birth.

Act Four: The heavenly host

Bible link

That night in the fields near Bethlehem some shepherds were guarding their sheep. All at once an angel came down to them from the Lord, and the brightness of the Lord's glory flashed around them. The shepherds were frightened. But the angel said, 'Don't be afraid! I have good news for you, which will make everyone happy. This very day in King David's home town a Saviour was born for you. He is Christ the Lord. You will know who he is, because you will find him dressed in baby clothes and lying on a bed of hay.'

Suddenly many other angels came down from heaven and joined in praising God. They said: 'Praise God in heaven! Peace on earth to everyone who pleases God.'

After the angels had left and gone back to heaven, the shepherds said to each other, 'Let's go to Bethlehem and see what the Lord has told us about.' They hurried off and found Mary and Joseph, and they saw the baby lying on a bed of hay.

When the shepherds saw Jesus, they told his parents what the angel had said about him. Everyone listened and was surprised. But Mary kept thinking about all this and wondering what it meant.

As the shepherds returned to their sheep, they were praising God and saying wonderful things about him. Everything they had seen and heard was just as the angel had said.

LUKE 2:8–20

Script

Reader 1:   That same night, on a hillside overlooking Bethlehem, shepherds were sitting quietly around a campfire watching their sheep. The night was calm and still as they gazed thoughtfully into the flames. As they watched their sheep quietly grazing, little did they know that they had been chosen above princes and kings to be the very first to visit baby Jesus.

Song: Warm winds blowing

Reader 2:   Suddenly, the hillside was filled with a blinding light. As the shepherds cowered and held up their hands to shield their eyes, they could just make out the figure of an angel. In their fear the shepherds were speechless, but the angel said…

Reader 1:   Don't be afraid! I have good news for you, which will make everyone happy. This very day in King David's home town a Saviour was born for you. He is Christ the Lord. You will know who he is, because you will find him dressed in baby clothes and lying on a bed of hay.

Reader 2:	Suddenly many other angels came down from heaven and joined in praising God. They said…
Reader 1:	Praise God in heaven! Peace on earth to everyone who pleases God.
Reader 2:	After this, the angels left the shepherds alone, bewildered and excited. They said to each other, 'Let us go over to Bethlehem and see what the angels have told us about!'
Reader 1:	So with great excitement the shepherds hurried down the hillside towards the town of Bethlehem. Soon they found Mary and Joseph, and saw the newborn baby lying on a bed of hay, just as the angel had said. The shepherds told Mary and Joseph what the angel had said about Jesus. Everyone listened and was surprised, but Mary kept thinking about all this and wondering what it meant.
Reader 2:	As the shepherds returned to their sheep, they were praising God and saying wonderful things about him. Everything they had seen and heard was just as the angel had said.

Act Five: Travellers from afar

Bible link

When Jesus was born in the village of Bethlehem in Judea, Herod was king. During this time some wise men from the east came to Jerusalem and said, 'Where is the child born to be king of the Jews? We saw his star in the east and have come to worship him.'

When King Herod heard about this, he was worried, and so was everyone else in Jerusalem. Herod brought together the chief priests and the teachers of the Law of Moses and asked them, 'Where will the Messiah be born?'

They told him, 'He will be born in Bethlehem, just as the prophet wrote, "Bethlehem in the land of Judea, you are very important among the towns of Judea. From your town will come a leader, who will be like a shepherd for my people Israel."'

Herod secretly called in the wise men and asked them when they had first seen the star. He told them, 'Go to Bethlehem and search carefully for the child. As soon as you find him, let me know. I want to go and worship him too.'

The wise men listened to what the king said and then left. And the star they had seen in the east went on ahead of them until it stopped over the place where the child was. They were thrilled and excited to see the star.

When the men went into the house and saw the child with Mary, his mother, they knelt down and worshipped him. They took out their gifts of gold, frankincense, and myrrh and gave them to him.

MATTHEW 2:1–11

Script

Reader 1:	Meanwhile, far away in the east, probably in the country then known as Persia, some wise astrologers were studying the stars when they noticed a bright new star in the sky. They believed that this star signified the birth of a new king. The wise men decided to follow the star in search of the new king.
Reader 2:	When Jesus was born in the village of Bethlehem in Judea, Herod was king. When the wise men arrived in Jerusalem, they said…
Reader 1:	Where is the child born to be king of the Jews? We saw his star in the east and have come to worship him.
Reader 1:	When King Herod heard about this, he was worried, and so was everyone else in Jerusalem. Herod brought together the chief

	priests and the teachers of the Law of Moses and asked them…
Reader 2:	Where will the Messiah be born?
Reader 1:	They told him, 'He will be born in Bethlehem, just as the prophet wrote, "Bethlehem in the land of Judea, you are very important among the towns of Judea. From your town will come a leader, who will be like a shepherd for my people Israel."'
Reader 2:	Herod secretly called in the wise men and asked them when they had first seen the star. He told them…
Reader 1:	Go to Bethlehem and search carefully for the child. As soon as you find him, let me know. I want to go and worship him too.
Reader 2:	The wise men listened to what the king said and then left. The star they had seen in the east went on ahead of them until it stopped over the place where the child was. They were thrilled and excited to see the star. When the men went into the house and saw the child with Mary, his mother, they knelt down and worshipped him. They took out their gifts of gold, frankincense and myrrh, and gave them to him.
Reader 2:	Gold is a gift fit for a king.
Reader 1:	Frankincense symbolises life and is used in prayer.
Reader 2:	Myrrh is a reminder of our mortality and is used to anoint the body after death.

Reader 1:	All three gifts speak of who Jesus is: King of kings, God's only Son, fully human and fully divine.
Reader 2:	Emmanuel—God is with us.

Song: Our Lord Emmanuel

Act Six (optional): Escape to Egypt

Bible link

Later they were warned in a dream not to return to Herod, and they went back home by another road.

After the wise men had gone, an angel from the Lord appeared to Joseph in a dream and said, 'Get up! Hurry and take the child and his mother to Egypt! Stay there until I tell you to return, because Herod is looking for the child and wants to kill him.'

That night, Joseph got up and took his wife and the child to Egypt, where they stayed until Herod died. So the Lord's promise came true, just as the prophet had said, 'I called my son out of Egypt.'
MATTHEW 2:12–15

Script

Reader 1:	Jesus has been born. The shepherds have been to visit him and the wise men have brought their gifts of gold, frankincense and myrrh, but Mary and Joseph are in danger. Because the wise men visited his palace in Jerusalem, King Herod knows that Jesus has been born and he sees the tiny baby as a threat to his own position as king. His final words to the wise men had been…
Reader 2:	Go to Bethlehem and search carefully for the child. As soon as you find him, let me know. I want to go and worship him too.
Reader 1:	The wise men were suspicious of Herod's slippery words. How could they trust him?

Song: Trust me

Reader 1: They were warned in a dream not to return to Herod, and they went back home by another road. But as they left, Joseph and Mary were still in great danger: Herod would stop at nothing to be rid of Jesus. After the wise men had gone, an angel from the Lord appeared to Joseph in a dream and said…

Reader 2: Get up! Hurry and take the child and his mother to Egypt! Stay there until I tell you to return, because Herod is looking for the child and wants to kill him.

Reader 1: That night, Joseph got up and took his wife and the child to Egypt, where they stayed until Herod died.

Reader 2: When Herod saw that he had been tricked by the wise man, he was furious. He ordered his soldiers to kill all the boys in and around Bethlehem who were two years old or under.

Reader 1: Herod's cruelty and wickedness came too late: Mary and Joseph had taken Jesus and escaped to the safety of Egypt.

Songs: Trust me (optional reprise); Take my hand (optional reprise)

Cue cards

Assembly One: God's chosen king

Jewish people: We remember the good old days. If only there was someone from David's line to help us now!'

Assembly Two: The annunciation

Angel: (1) You are truly blessed! The Lord is with you.

(2) Don't be afraid! God is pleased with you, and you will have a son. His name will be Jesus. He will be great and will be called the Son of God Most High. The Lord God will make him king, as his ancestor David was. He will rule the people of Israel for ever, and his kingdom will never end.

(3) The Holy Spirit will come down to you, and God's power will come over you. So your child will be called the holy Son of God. Your relative Elizabeth is also going to have a son, even though she is old. No one thought she could ever have a baby, but in three months she will have a son. Nothing is impossible for God!

Mary: (1) How can this happen? I am not married!

(2) I am the Lord's servant! Let it happen as you have said.

Assembly Three: The journey to Bethlehem

Augustus: I decree that there shall be a census! Every adult shall return to the town of their birth to be counted. All shall obey! By decree of the mighty Augustus!

Joseph: Do you have anywhere for us to stay? We have travelled a long way and the time for Mary's baby to be born is getting close.

Innkeepers: Sorry, no room here…

Assembly Four: The heavenly host

Angel: Don't be afraid! I have good news for you, which will make everyone happy. This very day in King David's home town a Saviour was born for you. He is Christ the Lord. You will know who he is, because you will find him dressed in baby clothes and lying on a bed of hay.

All angels: Praise God in heaven! Peace on earth to everyone who pleases God.

 Reproduced with permission from *Emmanuel… assemblies for Christmas* published by BRF 2010 (978 1 84101 624 5) www.barnabasinschools.org.uk

Assembly Five: Travellers from afar

Wise men: Where is the child born to be king of the Jews? We saw his star in the east and have come to worship him.

Wise man 1: Gold—the most precious and noble metal. It doesn't rust or tarnish and stays always bright, the true gift for a king.

Wise man 2: Frankincense—burnt to release its scented smoke. A symbol of life and rejuvenation.

Wise man 3: Myrrh—used in the embalming process, to prepare the body after death. A symbol of Jesus' own death, even at his birth!

Wise men: Where is the child born to be king of the Jews? We saw his star in the east and have come to worship him.

Herod: (1) Where will the Messiah be born?

(2) Go to Bethlehem and search carefully for the child. As soon as you find him, let me know. I want to go and worship him too.

Assembly Six (optional): Escape to Egypt

Herod: (1) I've heard about a new king being born somewhere in Bethlehem—and I don't like it! I will *not* have a threat to my royal throne! This new king is in deep trouble! Even if I have to kill all the baby boys in the area, there shall be no king but me!

(2) Go to Bethlehem and search carefully for the child. As soon as you find him, let me know. I want to go and worship him too.

Angel: Get up! Hurry and take the child and his mother to Egypt! Stay there until I tell you to return, because Herod is looking for the child and wants to kill him.

Music scores

We are here to sing to you

(Optional introductory song)

I can't see and I can't hear, but I know there's some - thing
know that it's a sign that it's near - ly Christ - mas

Words and music copyright © Mark Baxter 2009

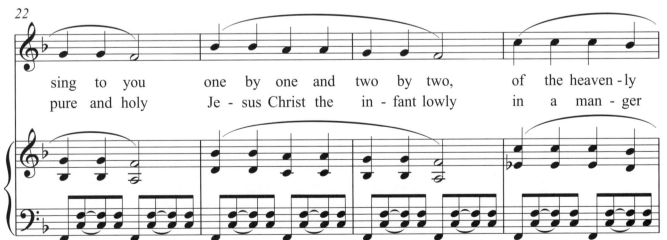

Words and music copyright © Mark Baxter 2009

We are here to sing to you one by one and two by two

of the heaven - ly king that's born, born our sav - iour

on this Christ - mas morn!

mf

Song 1: Take my hand

Words and music copyright © Mark Baxter 2000

Words and music copyright © Mark Baxter 2009

crys - tal___ snow, you think that I don't know the way you're feel - ing.
win - dow___ pane, an- oth - er year will wane in glow - ing em - bers.

p Don't be scared, don't you hide, I am close by your
Don't be scared, don't you hide, I am close by your

Vocal 1
side. *f* Take my hand. Take my___
side. Take my hand. Take my___

Vocal 2
f Take my hand. Take my

Words and music copyright © Mark Baxter 2009

Words and music copyright © Mark Baxter 2000

Believe in me.

Believe in me.

mf List-en to the sing-ing of the child-ren in the street.

mf List-en to the sing-ing of the child-ren in the street.

Mer-ry Christ-mas greet-ing all the peo-ple that they meet.

Mer-ry Christ-mas greet-ing all the peo-ple that they meet.

Words and music copyright © Mark Baxter 2009

Song 2: Mary's Song

Words and music copyright © Mark Baxter 2009

Words and music copyright © Mark Baxter 2009

Words and music copyright © Mark Baxter 2009

Song 3: Keep on ridin'

Words and music copyright Mark Baxter 2009

Words and music copyright Mark Baxter 2009

CHORUS

So keep on ri - din'__ a - long down this old du - sty trail

So keep on ri - din'__ so keep on won - drin'__ all day.

So keep on ri - din'__ a - long down this old du - sty trail

So keep on ri - din' so keep on won - drin'__ whe - hey!__

Words and music copyright Mark Baxter 2009

Words and music copyright Mark Baxter 2009

Words and music copyright Mark Baxter 2009

Song 4: Warm winds blowing

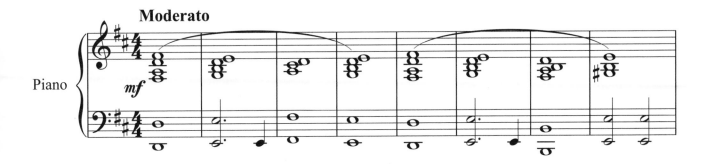

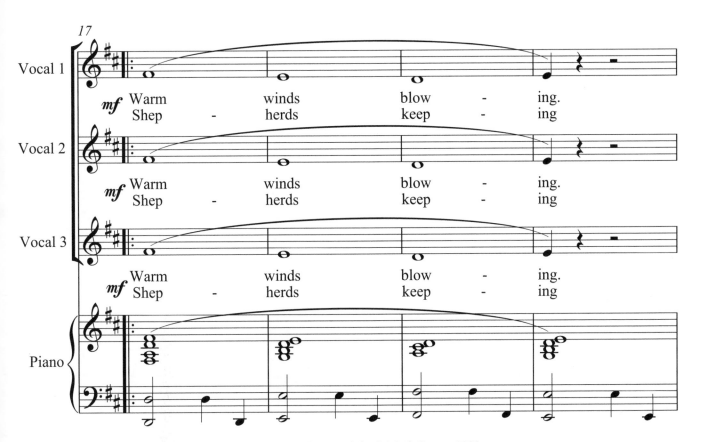

Words and music copyright © Mark Baxter 2009

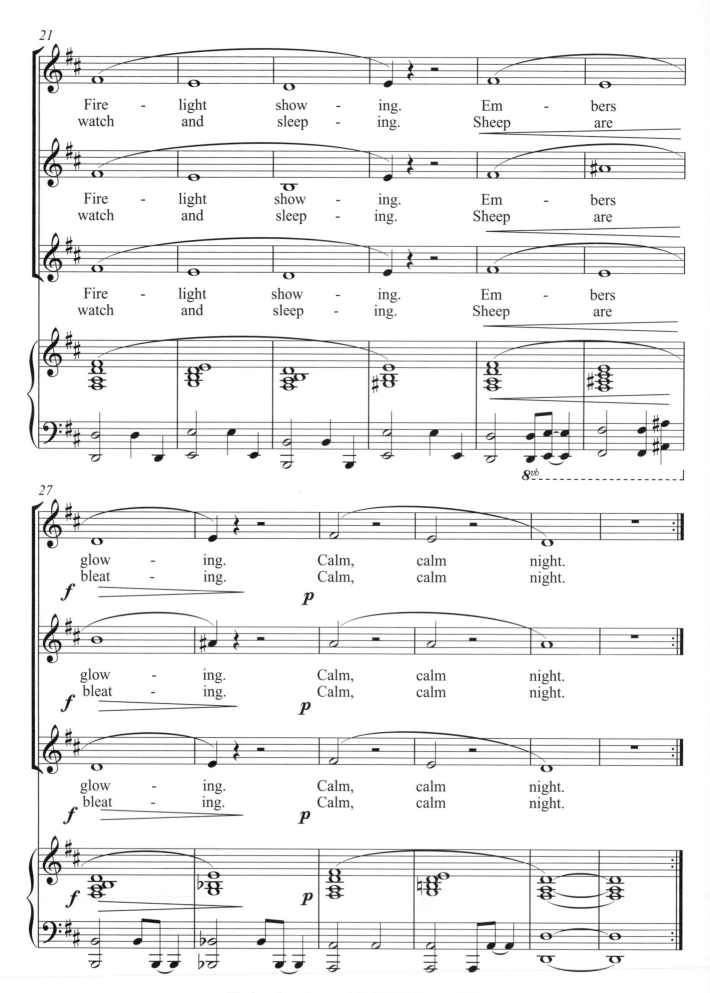

Words and music copyright © Mark Baxter 2009

 Reproduced with permission from *Emmanuel... assemblies for Christmas* published by BRF 2010 (978 1 84101 624 5) www.barnabasinschools.org.uk

Words and music copyright © Mark Baxter 2009

Words and music copyright © Mark Baxter 2009

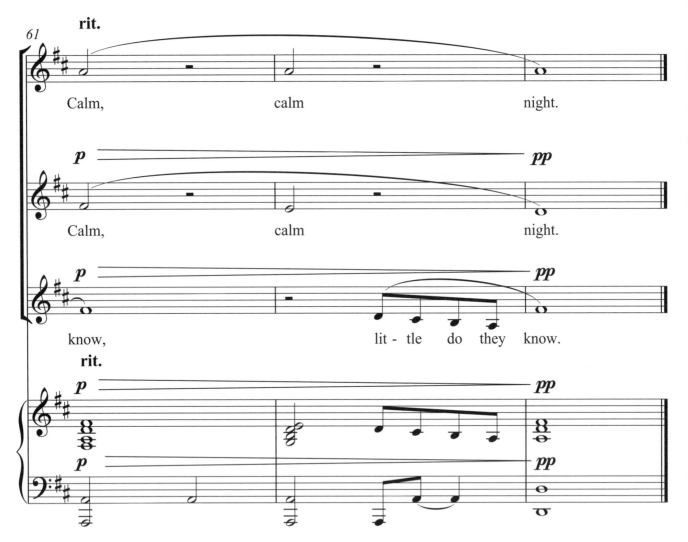

Words and music copyright © Mark Baxter 2009

Song 5: Our Lord Emmanuel

Long a - go the prophets fore-told Ma-ny years a - go Je - sus would come to save us all, our
Gold we bring, a gift for a king! Fran-kin - cense so rare! Fol-low the star to where it will rest, and

Words and music copyright © Mark Baxter 2009

Words and music copyright © Mark Baxter 2009

Words and music Copyright © Mark Baxter 2009

tell!_____ And great shall be____ the name we sing, Our Lord Em - man-__u - el!_____ And

tell!_____ And great shall be____ the name we sing, Our Lord Em - man-__u - el!_____ And

great shall be____ the name we sing, Our Lord Em - man-__u - el! _____ el!_____

great shall be____ the name we sing, Our Lord Em - man-__u - el! _____ el!_____

Words and music copyright © Mark Baxter 2009

Song 6: Trust me

Words and music copyright © Mark Baxter 2009

Words and music copyright © Mark Baxter 2009

Story Assemblies
for the School Year

36 assemblies with five-minute stories, teacher's notes and RE follow-up

Edward J. Carter

This book is full of memorable stories, designed to engage and delight pupils at primary level. The stories are essentially parables about God and the events in the Bible, creatively told to help children understand the big story of God's love for the world. Pupils are invited to imagine themselves as part of the story and also encouraged to think about their own values and behaviour, not by learning the right answers to give, but by making a leap of imagination and identifying themselves with the characters in the stories.

There are six themes in total, each with its own easy-to-make storytelling prop. The stories within each theme are divided into six weekly episodes, covering a wide range of contemporary values and topics. Together the stories cover the whole school year, with a key theme and a story in six parts for each half-term period. At the end of each half-term there is a special assembly to mark that part of the school year: harvest, Christmas, Christingle or Pancake Day, Holy Week or Easter, Pentecost, and a leavers' farewell.

As well as being ideal for collective worship, there are practical follow-up ideas to help children connect with the stories in the classroom. Alongside those in the book, there are further curriculum links on the website, www. barnabasinschools.org.uk/schools6993.

The six themes cover:

- God's creation
- The message of the Old Testament prophets
- Stories about Christian values
- The story of Holy Week and Easter
- Jesus' resurrection and ascension
- The journeys of the apostle Paul

ISBN 978 1 84101 699 3   £8.99
To order a copy of this book, please visit www.barnabasinschools.org.uk or use the order form opposite.

ORDERFORM

REF	TITLE	PRICE	QTY	TOTAL
699 3	Story Assemblies for the School Year	£8.99		

POSTAGE AND PACKING CHARGES				
Order value	UK	Europe	Surface	Air Mail
£7.00 & under	£1.25	£3.00	£3.50	£5.50
£7.10–£30.00	£2.25	£5.50	£6.50	£10.00
Over £30.00	FREE	prices on request		

Postage and packing	
Donation	
TOTAL	

Name _____   Account Number _____

Address _____

_____ Postcode _____

Telephone Number_____

Email _____

Payment by: ❑ Cheque ❑ Mastercard ❑ Visa ❑ Postal Order ❑ Maestro

Card no ▢▢▢▢ ▢▢▢▢ ▢▢▢▢ ▢▢▢▢ ▢▢▢

Valid from ▢▢▢▢   Expires ▢▢▢▢   Issue no. ▢▢▢

Security code* ▢▢▢   *Last 3 digits on the reverse of the card.
ESSENTIAL IN ORDER TO PROCESS YOUR ORDER   Shaded boxes for Maestro use only

Signature _____ Date _____

All orders must be accompanied by the appropriate payment.

Please send your completed order form to:
BRF, 15 The Chambers, Vineyard, Abingdon OX14 3FE
Tel. 01865 319700 / Fax. 01865 319701 Email: enquiries@brf.org.uk

❑ Please send me further information about BRF publications.

Available from your local Christian bookshop.   BRF is a Registered Charity

About
brf:

BRF is a registered charity and also a limited company, and has been in existence since 1922. Through all that we do—producing resources, providing training, working face-to-face with adults and children, and via the web—we work to resource individuals and church communities in their Christian discipleship through the Bible, prayer and worship.

Our Barnabas children's team works with primary schools and churches to help children under 11, and the adults who work with them, to explore Christianity creatively and to bring the Bible alive.

To find out more about BRF and its core activities and ministries, visit:

www.brf.org.uk
www.brfonline.org.uk
www.barnabasinschools.org.uk
www.barnabasinchurches.org.uk
www.messychurch.org.uk
www.foundations21.org.uk

If you have any questions about BRF
and our work, please email us at

enquiries@brf.org.uk